DISCOVER!

PEOPLE of the PAST

WHO WAS PAUL REVERE?

Robert Clore

Enslow PUBLISHING

Please visit our website, www.enslow.com. For a free color catalog of all our high-quality books, call toll free 1-800-398-2504 or fax 1-877-980-4454.

Cataloging-in-Publication Data
Names: Clore, Robert.
Title: Who was Paul Revere? / Robert Clore.
Description: Buffalo, NY : Enslow Publishing, 2027. | Series: People of the past | Includes glossary.
Identifiers: ISBN 9781978550537 (pbk.) | ISBN 9781978550544 (library bound) | ISBN 9781978550551 (ebook)
Subjects: LCSH: Revere, Paul, 1735-1818–Juvenile literature. | Statesmen–Massachusetts–Biography–Juvenile literature. | Massachusetts–History–Revolution, 1775-1783–Juvenile literature.
Classification: LCC F69.R43 C657 2027 | DDC 973.3311092 B–dc23

Published in 2027 by
Enslow Publishing
2544 Clinton Street
Buffalo, NY 14224

Designer: Claire Vanden Branden
Editor: Max Pritchard

Photo Credits: Cover, p. 1 Ian Dagnall Computing/Alamy; p. 5 Everett Collection/Shutterstock.com; pp. 7, 13, 15 Library of Congress; pp. 9, 11 Wikimedia Commons; p. 17 Internet Archive; p. 19 National Army Museum; p. 21 Sean Pavone/Shutterstock.com.

Printed in China

CPSIA compliance information: Batch #QS27ENS: For further information contact Enslow Publishing, at 1-800-398-2504.

CONTENTS

BOLDFACE WORDS APPEAR IN THE GLOSSARY.

AMERICAN PATRIOT

Paul Revere was an American **patriot**. Like many patriots of his time, he wanted America to be free from British rule. He played an important role early in the **American Revolution**.

EARLY LIFE

Paul was born on January 1, 1735. He lived in Boston, Massachusetts. During this time, Massachusetts was a British **colony**. It was one of 13 British colonies in North America.

PAUL REVERE'S FAMILY HOME

Paul's father was a **smith** who worked with gold and silver. He taught Paul to make forks and spoons, tea sets, and other objects. Paul even learned to use silver to replace missing teeth. Paul took over the business after his father died.

In 1756, Paul joined the armed forces of Massachusetts. The colonies were fighting for England in the French and Indian War. Paul fought in New York. The next year, he married Sarah Orne. She later died. Paul married Rachel Walker in 1773. He had 16 children.

A BATTLE IN THE FRENCH AND INDIAN WAR

RESISTING BRITISH RULE

In 1770, Paul created a famous **engraving** of the Boston **Massacre**. British soldiers had fired into a crowd of patriots. In 1773, a group of angry colonists threw British tea into Boston Harbor. This was called the Boston Tea Party. Paul was there! He and other patriots were unhappy with British **taxes** on tea.

By 1775, many colonists wanted revolution. Paul and others planned to warn their leaders if the British army was coming. Paul would carry a message. He had already been carrying messages between New York and Philadelphia.

PATRIOT LEADER SAMUEL ADAMS

PAUL REVERE'S RIDE

On the night of April 18, 1775, Paul learned the British army was coming to find two leaders of the revolution. He had to warn them! Paul crossed the Charles River by boat. He snuck past a British warship. Then he rode a horse to Lexington, Massachusetts.

Because of Paul's warning, the leaders escaped. Paul warned patriot soldiers. They gathered to meet the marching British army. This led to the Battles of Lexington and Concord. They were the first battles of the American Revolution.

THE BATTLE OF LEXINGTON

REMEMBERED WITH A POEM

Paul died in 1818. In 1860, a writer named Henry Wadsworth Longfellow wrote a **poem** about Paul. It was called "Paul Revere's Ride." Today, many people still read about Paul's famous ride!

A STATUE IN HONOR OF PAUL IN BOSTON

GLOSSARY

American Revolution: The war in which American colonists overthrew British control in order to choose a government run by the people.

colony: A piece of land under the control of another country.

engraving: Art carved onto a flat surface.

massacre: The killing of a large group of people, especially defenseless ones.

patriot: A colonist who rebelled against British control during the American Revolution.

poem: A piece of writing in verse that sometimes tells a story.

revolution: The overthrow of a government.

smith: A person who works with metals.

taxes: Money the government collects from the people.

FOR MORE INFORMATION

Books

Braun, Eric. *Battling for a New Nation at Lexington and Concord.* North Mankato, MN: Capstone Press, 2025.

Smith, Elliott. *Hidden Heroes in the Revolutionary War.* Minneapolis, MN: Lerner Publications, 2023.

Websites

The Paul Revere House
paulreverehouse.org
Learn more about Paul Revere and where he lived.

Paul Revere's Ride
poets.org/poem/paul-reveres-ride
Read Longfellow's poem about Paul Revere's famous ride.

INDEX